prescri for happiness

D0370810

ken keyes, jr.

LIVING LOVE PUBLICATIONS

This book is not copyrighted. It was written as a gift to our world that is suffering from separateness, noncooperation, strife and unhappiness. To keep prices low, the author receives no royalties on this book or any of his books listed in the back.

Anyone on the planet may reproduce this book in whole or in part without permission. It would be appreciated if acknowledgment is given in the following form:

ISBN 0-915972-02-6

Library of Congress Catalog Card Number
80-84855

Distributed to the book trade by

DeVorss & Company
P.O. Box 550
Marina del Rey, CA 90291

This book may be obtained through your local bookstore. Or you may order it from Living Love Publications, St. Mary, Kentucky 40063, for $2.00 plus 75¢ for postage and packing. (Kentucky residents add 5% for sales tax.)

To all my students
whose support
and dedication to their growth
help me learn about
and pass on the
Science of Happiness—
and to all those
whose open and inquiring minds
will someday bring
these effective principles
into their lives.

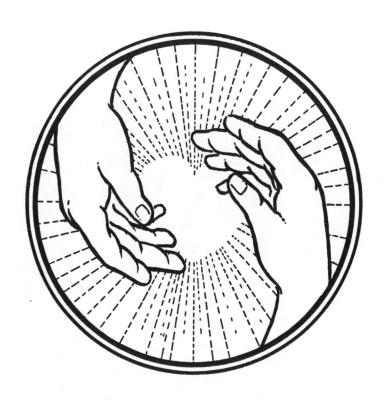

I guess you know.

You have been shortchanging yourself.

You've been depriving yourself
of just about everything
that's really worth having in life—

ENERGY

INSIGHT

PERCEPTIVENESS

LOVE

PEACE OF MIND

JOY

WISDOM

AND A DEEP FEELING OF PURPOSE.

If it's any consolation,
most likely
everybody else you know
has been lousing up
his or her life,
too.

But you don't have to
keep on adding
to the dismal statistics
of unhappiness:

a life without much warmth and love,
worrying about money,
pushing yourself to do your job,
a turned-off marriage,
divorce, anxiety,
sexual restlessness,
boredom, loneliness,
fear, resentment, hatred,
frustration, anger, worry,
jealousy, irritation,
headaches, ulcers
and high blood pressure,
plus a general feeling
of queasiness and uneasiness
about everything
from your bank account
to the nuclear bomb.

Why
punish yourself
any longer?

You've been blaming
it all on others—
or on yourself.

But a part of you knows
it's only some
unskillful habit patterns
of your mind
that constantly set you up
for creating unhappiness
time after time!

Really look at
what you're doing
to yourself.

Is it possible
for you
to live a joyous
and happy life
with peace of mind
in our topsy-turvy world?

Yes Yes Yes Yes Yes Yes Yes

Yes Yes Yes Yes Yes Yes Yes Yes

Yes Yes Yes Yes Yes Yes Yes Yes

Yes Yes Yes Yes Yes Yes Yes Yes

Yes Yes Yes Yes Yes Yes Yes Yes

IF—

This is a big IF.

Are you ready for it?

You can be happy

IF

you use the three
Prescriptions for Happiness
explained in this book.

These three prescriptions
really work.

They'll work
even if
you don't think
they'll work.

You may be telling yourself
that there is no way
they could work
in one of your life situations . . . .

But if you just take
these three prescriptions
and use them,
they will work for you
every time.

They're simple to understand.

They work—
if you do!

However, there is something
that will get in the way
of your applying them
in specific life situations
when you
most need them.

That something is you!

**Actually
it's
not
really
you . . . .**

It's only your mental habits,
and your selected memories
of how you think things are
that keep you from
molding things in your life
in a more harmonious way.

It's pride or
silly models of prestige
that get in your way.

Sometimes your mind would rather
prove itself right
than let you be happy!

But with practice,
you can learn
to handle these impediments.

I know you really want
to live a happy life.

We all do.

So let's get to work.

Here's the first of the three Prescriptions for Happiness:

KEN KEYES
Happiness Doctor

R

ASK FOR WHAT YOU WANT—
BUT DON'T DEMAND IT.

Use liberally as needed.
Memorize this prescription
so that you'll always have it
whenever you need it.

Refills: Anytime.

You stand a better chance
of getting what you want
when you ask for it
than when you don't.

That's obvious.

Why do you
often fail to ask
for what you want?

Sometimes you're afraid
that people
will be mad
at you
if you do.

Sometimes you hesitate
to assert yourself.

Perhaps you expect people
to read your mind.

Maybe you are practicing up
to become a martyr.

It's very simple—
just learn to ask
for what you want.

You don't have to pussyfoot
or play nicey-nicey.

You don't have to scream or yell.

You don't have
to fire up your mind
and make people
terribly wrong
if they don't do
what you ask.

You don't have to clam up.

You don't have
to retreat into
a deafening silence
that puts your relationship
into a deep freeze.

Just simply
ask for what you want—

without playing deceptive games,

without loading it down
with separating emotions
or implied threats,

without using
a heavy tone of voice.

Simply
but definitely
and specifically,
ask for
what you want!

Practice asking
for what you want
by noticing
how simply and directly
you can make requests
such as,
"Please pass the pepper,"
or
"Will you lock the door
when you leave?"

You'll be getting
the hang of it
when you can
ask for ANYTHING
in the same tone of voice
and with the same ease
as when you ask someone
to pass the pepper
or lock the door.

You will have to
practice a bit—
lots of bits!

You won't always find it easy
to ask for
money,
love,
sex,
or no sex,
assistance of various kinds
in a simple
yet specific
no-big-deal way.

Being simple,
direct and specific,
without making
a pressure-cooker situation
out of asking
for what you want
is a skill
you will have to develop
if you want to live
a happier life.

Now let's look at
the second part of the prescription:
"but don't demand it."

A demanding act comes from
a demanding frame of mind.

Look at your separating feelings,
your attitudes and mental positions.

And then see how you
act out your demands:
by playing "poor me,"
by playing "you hurt me" and
by playing "if you really loved me . . . ."
and on and on.

This will take
a lot of practice
because we're all so used
to demanding
so many things.

Remember, you can demand
with a forceful tone
or with silent pursed lips.

It's your vibrations that count!

24

Why do you
automatically demand
so much?

You're afraid people
won't treat you right
if you're not demanding.

You're afraid people
will run all over you.

So you make yourself very cactusy.

You're sure you're right—
and you want your rights
even if
you make yourself unhappy
getting your rights!

You feel that
when you spend
a lot of time with someone,
you'd better
shape up the person
so he or she
will fit your models!

But are you making
yourself happier
with all this demanding?

Do you really get
what you most want
in your life
through your demanding?

Are you really ready
to look
at how you are
addictively demanding
so many things of yourself,
of other people
and the world?

If you look closely
at the results you've had
from all the demanding
you've done recently,
I think you'll conclude
that even though
you're right,
the results you get
from demanding
are not all that good.

In other words,
most of the demanding you do
doesn't add
to your happiness.

You lose more happiness
than you gain.

You may discover
that a lot
of what you get
does not come
because of
your demanding it.

Why does it come?

It comes
because
it comes.

You're a part
of it all.

You have a right
to be here.

Sometimes you get
what you want
by demanding.

But it's like
losing a dollar
and gaining
a quarter!

When you either
loudly or softly demand
(instead of prefer)
you will lose:
insight,
humor,
enjoyment,
a feeling of love
(for yourself and others)
and your
peace of mind.

You've cheated yourself.

You never deserve
to be cheated by yourself.

How do you stop demanding?

It will mean loosening
the tight grip
YOU FEEL INSIDE YOU.

It will mean softening
the tones of your voice.

It will mean letting go
of that rock-like stance
you put on
when you ask for something.

It will mean that you
stop frowning
and feeling so serious
about the soap opera
we call life.

You'll probably
find it scary at first.
But with practice
it will be very relaxing
when you learn to ask for
what you want
without demanding.

It will mean taking the
this-is-such-a-heavy-problem tone
out of your requests—
along with all
the threatening
and worried
overtones.

It will mean sometimes
asking for things
with a smile and a feeling of fun
showing that
you're tuned-in
to the way life
is just a cosmic joke
after all!

Non-demanding means
that you learn
to ask lightly—
often humorously.

It's like you're
playing the game
of trying to get
what you want—
but you're well aware
that you win some
and you lose some.

And it's O.K. to lose.

You can be a good sport
about the game of life.

Asking for what you want
without demanding
means that you stop hinting
about what you want.

It means that you don't put things
so obliquely that people will have to
try to figure out what you want.

It means you stop going around
with a heavy disposition
hoping someone will ask you
what's the matter.

It means you quit downing yourself
by deciding in advance
that people won't want
to give it to you
or that you don't deserve
to get what you want.

It means that you learn
to ask again
for what you want TODAY—
even though you asked yesterday
without results.

Each day is
a new day.

You don't let
your memories of the past
hang over
and cloud up
the beautiful day
YOU CAN CREATE TODAY.

Now you're getting the hang of Prescription No. 1:

"Ask for what you want— but don't demand it."

That's the first of the three Prescriptions for Happiness.

Here's the second Prescription for Happiness:

KEN KEYES
Happiness Doctor

===

℞.

ACCEPT WHATEVER HAPPENS —
FOR NOW.

Memorize this prescription
so that you'll always have it
whenever you need it.

Refills: Anytime.

36

This second prescription
may be the toughest one
for you to use.

"Accept whatever happens—for now"
may mean
that you'll have to learn
to accept the "unacceptable."

You may have
to forgive the "unforgivable."

You may have
to love the "unlovable."

You'll have to learn
to get your finger off
that emergency alarm button
in your mind
that keeps you wound up
so tight inside.

Do you really think
your survival is threatened
by the stuff
you're clinging to
or running away from?

It means that
you'll have to tell your mind
that what looks like
a catastrophe—
just ain't so!

There are many
other people
who are emotionally accepting
what you're making yourself
unhappy about.

If they can
accept the "unacceptable,"
perhaps you can, too.

Can you give yourself
the insight
that it's your struggle
and your demanding
that's making you unhappy?

It's not whatever
you're struggling over.

It's your emotion-backed demand,
not the life situation itself,
that causes your experience
of unhappiness!

Make a list of
all the things
you couldn't stand
last year—
and the year before.

Some of them
you've now learned
to emotionally accept.

This is called growth.

You're too wonderful
to keep yourself
from growing more.

Most of your life problems
can no longer
be effectively handled
by primitive
"fight or flight"
responses.

You usually deprive yourself
of getting the most
from the people and situations
around you
when you come on with power
or let your fears
make you run away.

To develop the most
satisfying outcomes,
most of your problems
require more insight and a
practical back-and-forth
working with the situation
over a period of time.

Try to remember
that it's always your
emotion-backed demands
that are really
the practical cause
of your own unhappiness.

The art of happiness
means learning to be with
and to work and play with
the cast of characters
you've brought into
your life.

Retreating won't do it.

Coming on
like a ten-ton truck
won't do it,
either.

Emotionally accepting
and patiently working
with life situations
will get you
the most that's gettable!

Remember that a lot
of human suffering
is caused by the mind
that takes offense
at what's happening.

You don't have to respond
to ANYTHING
by taking offense.

You can learn to forgive yourself—
and others.

Accepting may mean that
you look at what you do have—
and quit focusing so much
on what you don't have.

You constantly throw yourself
out of the experience
of enoughness
because your mind
is continuously preoccupied
with what you don't have.

You don't let yourself enjoy
what you have
here and now
in your life.

It's ridiculous
what you keep doing
to yourself.

You have so much—
but you take it
for granted.

You constantly
make your happiness
dependent on
what you don't have—
or getting rid of
something you do have!

Do you have
enough air to breathe,
enough food and water and
some shelter from the elements?

Everything else
you're emotionally demanding
(and losing happiness over)
is a neurotic game
your mind
is playing with you.

How long
are you going to let
your mind
destroy your happiness?

Whenever
you turn your mind loose,
hankering after
what you don't have,
you keep on creating
the experience of unhappiness.

Whenever you direct your mind
into noticing and appreciating
the beautiful things
you always have,
there's no end
to the happiness
you will experience.

It's your choice—
how you operate
your mind—
and your life.

"Accept whatever happens—for now."

It doesn't mean you have to
like what's happening.

It doesn't mean you have to
stop trying to change
what's happening.

It doesn't mean you have to think
that whatever happens is right.

"Accept whatever happens—for now"
may mean:

You're going to stop
making yourself
so afraid, so angry,
so resentful, so worried—
and so unhappy.

You're going to prefer
that something be different—
but not addictively
demand it any longer!

You're going to change
your internal emotional experience.

Suppose you're mad at someone.

Do you hold on to your anger
because you believe
if you stopped being mad
it would make him or her
"right"?

Perhaps you need
more practice
in gently holding onto
what you feel is right
without creating anger
in yourself.

Do you hold onto
irritation and resentment
because you're embarrassed
to let go?

Look at all the uptightness
and tension
you're creating
in your body and mind.

Relax for your own sake.

You can enlarge your perspective.

You can let go of your negativity—
and your "me-vs.-you" resistance
even when you're right.

Does being upset
have to be
an unavoidable consequence
of being right?

When you're right,
you can be serene
and not lose
your peace of mind.

A skillful mind
can be right
in a given situation
and at the same time
let itself feel good
when people don't
agree with it.

To be happy
and feel good,
you can no longer afford
to let your mind
get away with criticalness
and disdainful judgmentalness
hiding under
a mask of politeness.

Let go of convincing others
that you're right—
and treat yourself
to happiness!

This accepting or letting go
is a sensitive
inner surrender—
not a forced
outer surrender.

INNER SURRENDER
is not based on
your feeling defeated.

It comes from

YOUR

OWN

INTELLIGENT

CHOICE.

It's based on INSIGHT—
not fear.

It's a wise decision
(even a purely selfish decision!)
that you make for yourself
to get more happiness
in your life.

It's a skill
you'll have to practice.

It does not
come easily
to the human mind.

The letting go,
the inner surrender,
the non-demanding
we are talking about
IS VASTLY DIFFERENT
from defeat,
or submissiveness,
or a loss of strength,
or diminished effectiveness,
or loss of individuality.

Notice that
when you're defeated,
you don't really let go
of your inner demand.

You just turn loose
of the bone
you were fighting over.

You're still tormented inside
by an inner desire
that dominates
your consciousness—
you are still demanding the bone.

What we're talking about is
YOUR RELEASING YOURSELF
FROM INNER DESIRES
for what the world
is not ready
to give you
right here
and right now.

Wisely letting go
saves your energy,
clears your mind,
gives you sharper insights,
enables you to enjoy
the here-and-now moment
in your life
and helps you
increase your love
for yourself
and all other people.

As you learn
to emotionally accept it all,
you will heal the
THREE BLEEDING SEPARATENESSES
that keep you from getting
the most from your life.

You'll unify your psyche,
often divided against itself—
(your mind vs. your mind)
repressing, judging, downing you
and creating unpleasant feelings.

You'll heal the
mind-vs.-body split
that destroys your aliveness
by rejecting or ignoring your body,
its by-products or its desires—
and makes you feel half-dead.

You'll no longer perpetuate
the me-vs.-others battle
that keeps you alienated from people
and destroys your joy of living.

This gentle letting go
of the demands
and attachments
of your mind
represents the highest level
of true strength
and character
in a human being.

Now let's look
at the last two words
in the second prescription.

What do we mean by
"for now"?

"For now" means "for now."

EVERYTHING IN LIFE CHANGES.

You'll be surprised
how often things
will change
and give you
what you want—
without your manipulating
or forcing them—
when you use the three
Prescriptions for Happiness.

"For now"
helps your mind
tune-in to
the here and now.

After all,
the here and now
is all
you've ever got.

You only have
the "now moment."

Yesterday is gathering dust
in the files of your brain.

And tomorrow is only a thought.

There will never be a tomorrow!

When tomorrow comes
it will always be "now."

That's why the
now moment
is "eternal"!

Don't give up
your now happiness,
thinking it will
all be better—
tomorrow.

It hasn't—
and it won't.

Now is it!
It's all you've got—ever.

Postponed happiness
may be
lost happiness.*

*alas!

So stop making yourself
so upset
because life is
the way it is.

In the precise here-and-now moment
there is nothing you can do
to change anything.

Maybe you can change it
one second from now—
or one month from now.

And it's O.K.
to play the game
of shaping things up
the way you want them.

JUST DON'T MAKE

YOURSELF UNHAPPY

IN THE MEANWHILE.

Why not be kind to yourself—
"for now"?

Relax your too-active mind.

Our minds stay so busy
regretting the dead past
and creating concern
about the imaginary future that
NOW IS CONTINUALLY LOST!

Enjoy what's now—
even though
a part of it
is not the way
you want it to be.

One of the things
you haven't been willing to face
is that your life
will never meet
your mental models of perfection.

It's always been "imperfect."

It always will be "imperfect."

That's the way life is.

If you want to be happy
you'll learn to be with life
and accept life
the way it is—
which means
it will sometimes fit your expectations—
and sometimes it won't.

Sometimes life is lousy.

BUT YOU DON'T HAVE TO
MAKE YOURSELF FEEL LOUSY.

If your mind
will look around
it will see
that it always
HAS ENOUGH
to be happy!

If you'll just PREFER
that things be different,
you can enjoy your life.

And you can put energy
into changing
what you don't like.

But quit demanding
that they be different
from the way they are now—
even if you're right!

In other words,
the happy person
learns to live
with the daily "imperfections"
of his or her life.

As you grow
in awareness
you'll discover
that it's all perfect—
either for your growth
or your enjoyment!

Sometimes
you won't want
to grow so fast!

Sometimes you can use the past
for your present growth.

Look back again
over what's happened
in your life
during the past year . . . .

Did all your uptightness,
did all your fear, anger, jealousy,
worry, resentment, grief,
irritation and heartbreak
solve your problems?

Replay in your mind
the heavy dramatic "acts"
in the soap opera of your life
during the past year.

Can you see
how you could have used
the second prescription
"accept whatever happens—for now"
in every one of those situations
and you would not have had
to make yourself
so upset and unhappy?

Always remember
that the purpose
of the second prescription
is to try
to instantly stop
the way you've been
making yourself unhappy
time after time,
day after day.

These Prescriptions for Happiness
show you how to change
YOUR EXPERIENCE OF LIFE ! ! !

If you do this
you can let yourself
enjoy your life
all the time—
even when things go
from bad to worse.

As you increase your skill
in using the three
Prescriptions for Happiness,
you can be happy
most of the time.

To enjoy your life
most of the time,
you've got to realize
that the world
hasn't been doing it to you!

You've been doing it yourself!

The world rolls on—
and does what it does.

But only you can create
YOUR EXPERIENCE
of your life.

Now let's summarize
some of the things
your mind may forget:

You can emotionally
"accept whatever happens—for now"
and at the same time
you do not have to like
what happens.

You can try to change
whatever is wisely changeable
without setting up
more problems in your life.

To emotionally accept
whatever happens
means that
you don't even have
to give up your feelings
that what is happening
is wrong!

You just give up
making yourself unhappy!

You can create
an enjoyable experience
of your life—
even when things
aren't the way
you'd like them to be.

And that begins to happen
when you learn to
"accept whatever happens—for now."

As long as you live,
you'll win some
and you'll lose some.

Your life
will sometimes seem "perfect"
and sometimes seem "imperfect."

Things will go up and down.

BUT YOUR EXPERIENCE OF LIFE

DOES NOT HAVE TO GO

UP AND DOWN !!!

Good luck.

**Remember, you can
master your mind
when the going gets rough.**

You're now ready
for the third
Prescription for Happiness:

KEN KEYES
Happiness Doctor

Rx

TURN UP YOUR LOVE—
EVEN IF YOU DON'T GET
WHAT YOU WANT.

To be used very liberally all the time.
Memorize this prescription. Even so,
you'll forget sometimes.

Refills: Every heart has an infinite supply—
whether it's used or not.

I'll bet you think
that the third
Prescription for Happiness
suggests that you
"turn up your love"
in order to be nice
to other people.

That's not it.

YOU TURN UP YOUR LOVE TO BE NICE TO YOURSELF!

Can you see
that you've been making yourself
separate and unhappy
because you've kept
your love turned off—
toward yourself
and other people?

What do we mean by love?

Love isn't kind acts
or gifts wrapped
with a bow on top—
although love may lead you
to do these things.

Love means
tearing down the separateness
and the boundaries
between your heart feelings
and another person.

Love is just
a feeling
of togetherness
and openness
in your heart.

Actually,
when you love someone
it means that
he or she
is putting you in touch
with a part of you
that you love
in yourself.

Conversely,
notice that when
you're rejecting someone,
he or she
is only doing
what you would strongly reject
in yourself!

The world is your mirror . . . .

Love is a feeling of closeness,
of warmth,
of nonseparateness,
of understanding,
of togetherness —
of oneness.

Love is not a matter
of what happens in life.

It's a matter of
what's happening
in your heart.

Most people
aren't very skillful
in loving.

They create difficulties
in loving themselves
and other people.

They think
that if they love someone,
they've got to like everything
the person says and does.

They think it means
they're obligated
to do something.

They think love means
you can't say "no"
to someone you love.

As a skillful lover
you can tell yourself
(and even others),

"Whether I like
what you do or say
has no effect on
whether I love you
or not.

"I don't have to love
your actions—

"IT'S YOU I LOVE."

To whatever degree
you have strings
attached to your love,
you're not really loving.

In other words
the game is to
"love everyone unconditionally—
including yourself."

Always remember,
love is a heart feeling—
it is not what you say or do
although your feeling of love
will definitely
have an influence
on many of your actions.

When you get right down to it—

You love a person
because he or she
is there.

This is the only reason.

You don't love people
because they desperately
want your love.

You don't love people
because they need it.

You don't love people
because they deserve it.

You don't love people
because you want them
to love you.

(Some may not
allow themselves
to love you.)

You just love them—
because they're there!

Notice that love doesn't work
as a barter or an exchange.

"I'll love you if you love me"
is usually ineffective.

Here's what works perfectly
to increase your happiness:

"I'll love you no matter
what you say or do.

"I'll love you always.

"No strings.

"No barter.

"No exchange.

"No bookkeeping.

"My love just is—
because we are here."

"I may not want
to be with you sometimes
because I don't like
the roles
that you play
in the soap opera
of life.

"But I'll always love you.

"I'll always
have that
heart-to-heart feeling
that I create in me
when I think
of you."

How do you increase
your feeling of love for people?

Hug them more often or
look into their eyes more deeply
to help you open up and experience
the human being that is there—
that is just trying,
skillfully or unskillfully,
to get his or her life
to work better.

Share with others
your most secret thoughts.

Experience everything
that everyone does or says
as though you had done or said it.

Help them in caring ways.

To love more deeply,
open your eyes to see and appreciate
the beauty that is in your own life.

Become more aware
(perhaps by making lists)
of the things that are lovable
about you and your world.

This will lead you automatically
into experiencing the beauty
and lovableness
of the people around you.

As you open your heart,
perhaps slowly at first,
you will soon discover
that people respond
by opening their hearts to you.

Before you know it
your love will be increasing
not as a word
or as another "should,"
but as a vital feeling
you create in your heart.

To increase your love
imagine that someone's heart
is inside your heart
and that both hearts
resonate together:

Put yourself in his or her shoes
so that you can understand—
with both your mind
and your heart.

Understanding
with your heart
gives you emotional contact
with another person.

Understanding
with your mind
means to honor and accept
the value of the lessons
life is offering
the other person.

Wisdom
is the compassionate blend
of both the
heart and mind.

Now let's look
at the second part
of the third prescription,
which says
to turn up your love
"even if you don't get what you want."

You don't need this prescription
to turn up your love
when you get what you want.

It's easy to love
when the sun is shining
and you're getting your way!

You don't need this book
to tell you how to be happy then.

To be a skillful lover
you must be able
to keep your own heart open
to another person
no matter what's happening
in the soap opera
of your life.

You can throw someone
out of your melodrama.

BUT DON'T THROW HIM OR HER

OUT OF YOUR HEART!

What you've got to learn
if you want to create
a happy life
is to
turn up your love
even when you're not
getting your way ! ★ ! # !

You'll have to practice this.
It doesn't come easily—
except with dogs.

Have you ever noticed
how often a dog
will wag its tail
and keep on loving you—
even if you don't
take it everywhere you go
or feed it on time?

A dog doesn't withhold love
to control you.

If you can train yourself
to make your love
as unconditional
as that of most dogs,
you'll have it made!

You really know this.

You just keep forgetting it.

Christ said, "Love one another."

Love is a central theme
in every religion.

Our lives are set up
to give us a head start
with a big dose
of unconditional mother-love
when we first
come into the world.

Your life
can be successful,
wealthy,
prestigious
and influential.

But it won't be enough.

You will not reach
your potential for happiness
unless you experience
a lot of love
for yourself and
for other human beings.

Love is more powerful
than all
the bombs on earth
put together.

Love can bring peace—
bombs will not.

People will do things freely
from the love in their hearts
that they would never do
without their love
no matter how much
you bribe
or threaten them.

All human beings
are either near
or distant relatives
to each other.

Our human-to-human love
that experiences all people
as "US"
is the only possible way
to bring peace,
harmony,
cooperativeness
and enjoyment of life
to the four billion people
on this earth.

We couldn't fight wars,
either personal
or international,
if we had
more love
in our hearts.

It's easy to love
those who love you.

But are you skilllful enough
to keep your love
turned up in your heart
even when you think
that other people are
hating you,
ridiculing you,
downing you,
refusing to be with you
or are doing things
to hurt you?

If you develop a high level of skill
in keeping your love turned up
(even when you don't get what you want),
you can elect yourself
a member of
the lovers' club!

Don't worry about whether
other people are loving you.

That's their problem.

As you increase your skill
in living a happy life,
your ONLY concern
will be whether YOU are
loving other people.

You can learn to put your love
on automatic
regardless of whether
they reflect back
your love.

You can always create
your own experience of life
in a beautiful and enjoyable way
if you keep your love
turned on within you—
regardless of what
other people say or do.

So let's go beyond ourselves.

We can learn
to turn up our love—
even when we don't
get what we want.

We can extricate ourselves
from the clashing
separate identities
we are so valiantly defending.

We can free ourselves
from who we think we are
so that the beautiful beings
we are deep inside
can come out and play
with the other beautiful beings
around us.

We've got to convince
our egos
and our minds
that if we want
to live happy lives,

love
is
more
important
than
anything
else!

S o now you've got
all three
Prescriptions for Happiness:

KEN KEYES
Happiness Doctor

1. ASK FOR WHAT YOU WANT—
   BUT DON'T DEMAND IT.

2. ACCEPT WHATEVER HAPPENS—
   FOR NOW.

3. TURN UP YOUR LOVE—
   EVEN IF YOU DON'T GET
   WHAT YOU WANT.

It takes skill and insight
to use these
Prescriptions for Happiness.

They're not as easy
as taking a pill.

You have to work with
your desire systems,
your ego,
your selective memory,
your mental habits
and your illusions
of your pride and prestige.

For the rest of your life
you'll need to work on yourself
using these prescriptions.

But it's a lot easier
than all the misery
and unhappiness
you put yourself through
when you ignore these
Prescriptions for Happiness.

It may take you months
or even years
to acquire the skill
to use these guidelines.

You've got to learn
to use them
in your heavier life situations—
which is the time when
you need them most.

So try not to let yourself
get discouraged—
and for your happiness' sake,
don't ever give up!

You probably
won't ever be able
to apply these prescriptions
perfectly.

You're not addicted
to always meeting your models,
are you?!?

You don't have to apply them perfectly.

The more you apply them,
the more you get the benefits.

Be content with more or less,
rather than all or none.

So now you've got it.

There's only one person
in the world
that can really
make you happy.

There is only one person
in the world
that can really
make you unhappy.

How about
getting to know
this person
more deeply?

For starters,
go look
in the mirror
and smile
and say,
"Hello."

And then tell yourself
that for a while
you're going to quit
putting so much energy
into trying to change
the people around you.

It hasn't worked
that well,
has it?

Instead,
you're going to put your energy
into doing the inner work
on your own mind
that will enable you
to use these
Prescriptions for Happiness
skillfully and effectively
in your daily life.

Life goes by rapidly.

Don't delay.

Don't put it off.

Don't wait until
you have some
spare time.

Don't wait until
the time's "right."

Don't let the mind
that you're trying to retrain
talk you out of doing it!

Your mind's
really good at this.

Your mind will come up
with lots of reasons
for not following
the three prescriptions.

Keep telling your mind
that you are determined
to do it!

Tell your mind
you want to live
a life characterized by:

ENERGY,

INSIGHT,

PERCEPTIVENESS,

LOVE,

PEACE OF MIND,

JOY,

WISDOM,

AND A FEELING OF PURPOSE.

Ask your mind to help you.

It's your friend, you know.

And if you're determined,
it will give you
what you want.

Do you really want
to use the prescriptions
or do you
just want to want
to do it?

Don't wait any longer
for the people around you
to make you happy.

Don't wait for the world
to fit your models
closely enough
so you can create
the experience
of peace and enjoyment.

HAPPINESS IS A DO-IT-YOURSELF GAME!

AND TIME IS PASSING!

Loving more
and demanding less

are not only
the nicest things
you can do
for yourself.

They're also
the most caring things
you can do
for the whole world!

These three prescriptions
are actually quite contagious.

The more you use them yourself,
the more the people around you
will use them—
even if you don't tell them
about the prescriptions.

They'll just pick them up.

And the children around you
will learn to use them
as automatically
as they absorb a language.

But here's
a word of caution:

Don't demand
that others use
these prescriptions.

Such demands
(even though you're right!)
will only
decrease your happiness.

Let them learn
BY YOUR EXAMPLE—
and not by
your preaching.

It can't be taught.

It has to be caught!

The effect of using the
Prescriptions for Happiness
will seem like
a miracle to you—
and perhaps to others.

Actually, miracles
are normal everyday events
for people who skillfully use
these principles
moment by moment
in their lives.

After all,
a miracle is something
you would like to have happen
that you didn't expect.

The results
in your life
that you will get
by using the
Prescriptions for Happiness
may seem
like miracles to you
because you've never tuned-in
to the real power of love.

Love helps things
get rearranged,
harmonized and settled
without our bruising
or harming each other.

B e sure to memorize the
Prescriptions for Happiness
so they'll be right there
when you need them:

1. Ask for what you want—
   but don't demand it.

2. Accept whatever happens—for now.

3. Turn up your love—
   even if you don't get what you want.

Don't let life
catch you
without these prescriptions.

They'll help you create
the happiest life
you can possibly have.

And remember,
you're always
beautiful,
capable and
lovable
even if you don't
always succeed
in using the three
Prescriptions for Happiness.

I love you,

Ken

Continuing Your Growth

If you want some help,
there's a lot of it available.

To begin with,
keep rereading this book.

It's all in here,
although you may not understand
how wonderfully it works
to unravel the knots
in your life
when you first read it.

Cornucopia is a college
that offers courses
from a weekend to a month
that give you actual practice
in creating a happy life
in everyday living situations—
in your marriage,
in your business
and in all areas
of your life.

Cornucopia
also offers
weekend workshops
in most of the larger cities
in the nation
from time to time.

By sending for a catalog
you can be tuned-in
to these workshops
that are happening
within a few minutes
or a few hours
from where you live.

To get more information
or a free catalog
you can
write or phone:

Cornucopia
St. Mary, Kentucky 40063
(502) 692-6006

These books will help you increase your skill in creating a happier life—

A Conscious Person's Guide to Relationships
by Ken Keyes, Jr. $3.95
This guide shows you how to use the techniques of Living Love to create a more delightful relationship with the person you have chosen to live with. Seven guidelines are offered for entering into a relationship. There are also seven guidelines for being in a relationship, and seven guidelines for decreasing your involvement in a relationship. It is enjoyable to read, realistic in its approach and immensely helpful if you have a relationship or wish to find one. It will show you how to gradually create the high level of love and enjoyment you've wanted to share with another person.

How to Enjoy Your Life in Spite of It All
by Ken Keyes, Jr. $4.95
Each of the Twelve Pathways is thoroughly explained in this book. Ken (who formulated the Twelve Pathways) offers you his detailed insights into these guidelines for creating a more enjoyable life. Step by step, he shows you how to take the Pathways from the printed page and make them dynamic tools for bringing increased energy, perceptiveness, love and inner peace into your day-to-day living.

Handbook to Higher Consciousness
by Ken Keyes, Jr. $2.95
This is the basic text in the Living Love system. It introduces
five Methods and the Consciousness Doubler for working on
your addictive demands. It has chapters on applying these life-
giving principles to different areas of your life. Countless people
have experienced that their lives have changed dramatically
from the time they began to use the practical methods explained
in the *Handbook to Higher Consciousness.*

How to Make Your Life Work or
Why Aren't You Happy?
by Ken Keyes, Jr. and Tolly $2.00
In this delightful introductory book, every other page is a car-
toon. It is ideal as a gift for people you want to introduce to
this helpful approach to expanding their lives.

Taming Your Mind
by Ken Keyes, Jr. $5.95 clothbound
This is an effective guide to making sound decisions. The helpful
"tools for thinking" are illustrated by 80 drawings by Ted Key.

**These books are available through bookstores or by mail
from Living Love Publications. Please enclose 75¢ per
book for postage and packaging. Kentucky residents add
5% for sales tax.**

**For information on other books, trainings, cassettes and
posters, or to have your name placed on the mailing list,
you may write to:**

Living Love Publications
St. Mary, Kentucky 40063

NEW LOCATION:
LIVING LOVE BOOKROOM
Ken Keyes Center
790 Commercial Ave
Coos Bay, OR 97420

COVER BY JOE PARKER
DRAWINGS BY MEG STUDER